INTRODUCTION

As the news came through that Britain was at war, the nation faced up to the inevitable battle ahead. Children were already being evacuated into the countryside, and gas masks had been issued the previous year (sometimes being used for other purposes). War journals began their picture-story coverage, in-house magazines like The New Bond (Woolworths) reported staff movements, and the propaganda poster campaign began to advise a worried public – 'Save Fuel for Battle' and 'Don't Listen to the Squander Bug, buy War Savings'.

It didn't take long for the entrepreneurs to see an opportunity – a 3d Globrite badge would help others see you in the dark, and the game of Spotto (played of course like lotto) combined fun with identifying friend from foe in the sky. From somewhere, Mr Chad (aka Mr Watno) nosed over the garden wall to see, amongst other things, that there were no bananas – a fact that had become sufficiently irksome by 1942 for two songs to be written bemoaning the fact. At this time, too, Gremlins had been found to be responsible for unexplained mechanical failures. Roald Dahl described the symptoms in his book for children.

BBC radio became the lifeline of the nation, primarily for its news broadcasts, but also for its classical music, light entertainment and helpful programmes on practical matters. Listeners came to rely on the Radio Doctor for his sensible advice, and on the Kitchen Front for tips on how to supplement the rations by bottling fruit, for instance, or serving rabbit stew with prune dumplings. For the record, by 1943 a week's ration for one included: 2oz of tea, 4oz of jam, 8oz of sugar, 3oz of sweets, 2oz of lard, 2oz of margarine, 2oz of butter, 4oz of bacon, 3/4lb of meat, and perhaps an egg if you were lucky.

The radio did have one nasty surprise – the traitor nicknamed Lord Haw Haw calling from Germany and broadcasting on the airwaves with worrying news and predictions. This could be countered by the Daily Mirror's Jane, the saucy heroine spy who regularly shed her clothes – the fewer the clothes, the harder the troops fought. But it was often British humour and determination that saw the job through – a blitzed shopkeeper's sign would say "More open than usual" and a barber next to a bombed building, "We've had a close shave, come and get one yourself".

When the AIR RAID warning goes— What shall we DO?

Issued by the A.R.P. Committee of SOUTHAMPTON
For the Protection of yourself and your family.

A Series of Charts giving full instructions as to Air Raid Precautions, Gas Effects and Recognition and Treatment of Injuries

ESSENTIAL TO FIRE WATCHERS

AIR RAID FIRST AID

AUTHORITATIVE
CLEAR · CONCISE · COMPLETE

6D

Eighth Impression

A.R.P.
HOME OFFICE · SCOTTISH OFFICE
MARCH · · · · 1938

THIS leaflet sets out the choices open to every British citizen who wishes to take his or her part in the voluntary national organisation of the Air Raid Precautions Services.

HOME OFFICE

THE PROTECTION OF YOUR HOME AGAINST AIR RAIDS

A·R·P
FOR LONDONERS

In the Opinion of the Experts only the Tunnel Scheme Can Give Real Protection

WAR TIME FIRST AID for EVERYMAN

E. G. BAILEY

S. EVELYN THOMAS'S
HANDY WAR-TIME GUIDE

FOR THE WOMAN AT HOME AND THE MAN IN THE STREET

HOW TO PROTECT YOUR HOME
FIRST AID IN AIR RAIDS
HOW TO DEAL WITH FIRE
WHAT TO DO ABOUT ANIMALS
IMPORTANT WAR REGULATIONS
WHAT TO KNOW ABOUT GAS MASKS
HOW TO STORE & PROTECT FOOD
WHAT TO DO IN THE BLACKOUT
HOW TO ECONOMISE IN WARTIME
WHAT TO DO IN AN AIR RAID

THIS LITTLE BOOK SHOULD BE IN EVERY HOME. IT WILL PROVE INVALUABLE IN EMERGENCY. IF YOU FIND IT USEFUL AND HELPFUL, PLEASE RECOMMEND IT TO YOUR FRIENDS.

6D

A CONCISE, FULLY ILLUSTRATED AND PRACTICAL GUIDE FOR THE HOUSEHOLDER AND AIR-RAID WARDEN
Officially recommended by The Air Raid Defence League

By S. EVELYN THOMAS

6D

JAMES ASKEW & SON
CORPORATION ST·, P

A.R.P.
HOME STORAGE OF FOOD SUPPLIES

What to buy and how to use

MINISTRY OF HOME SECURITY
1940

Air Raids

WHAT YOU MUST KNOW
WHAT YOU MUST DO

EXTRA PRECAUTIONS

EXTRA PRECAUTIONS AGAINST EXPLOSIVE BOMBS

TRENCHES. Instead of having a refuge-room in your house, you can, if you have a garden, build a dug-out or a trench. A trench provides excellent protection against the effects of a bursting bomb, and is simple to construct; but keep it away from the house to avoid falling débris. The danger to beware of is the danger of gas. Although the risk of a heavy concentration of gas is not...

COMPLETE AIR RAID PRECAUTION

A·B·C of A·R·P
ILLUSTRATING HOME OFFICE INSTRUCTIONS
6

SECOND (Revised and Enlarged) EDITI

A PICTURE GUIDE for Householders & A.R.P. Personnel

CONTENTS include—

Air Raid Warnings
Construction of Shelters and Trenches
Notes on High Explosive
Precautions Against Incendiary Bombs
Poison Gas Tables
All about Gas Masks and Babies' Helmets
Gas-proof Clothing and Decontamination
Pets and Animals
Evacuation
Food Supplies
First Aid
Etc.

A.R.P.
THE PRACTICAL AIR RAID PROTECTION BRITAIN NEEDS

1d

AIR RAID PRECAUTION

* The A.R.P. Warden's Post for your Sector is :
ARP GROUP 31
39, Gilston Road
S.W.10

* The nearest First Aid Post is :
Brompton Hospital
Fulham Rd

* THESE TWO POSTS WILL ALWAYS BE MANNED DURING AIR RAIDS.

Help or advice upon A.R.P. matters will be [given] by the local wardens.

The nearest SENIOR WARDEN is:
Mr. Sargent
1 Harley Gdns.

Ask him for the name and address of your nearest local Warden and make a note of it here:
Mrs. McKnight
37 Cranley Gdns

Go to know him now and note any ch[anges] in the names and addresses given here.

Pictures SHOW YOU HOW IT'S DO
N & SONS LIMITED · 116 CHANCERY LANE · LONDON, W.

CHOICE OF ROOM

om 10 ft. × 10 ft. × 8 ft. will accommodate 5 persons for 12 hours.

best (if two exits) or basement or room on ground one with small windows, side of house, away from ailing wind, soft ground outside, or room close to aining house (Protection from H.E. Blast).

HOW TO MAKE A ROOM GAS-PROOF

Fill in all cracks with pulp made of sodden newspaper or putty, pasted over with strong "gummed" paper or brown paper, and paste afterwards.

FILL IN
A. & B.—Windows.
C. & D.—Doors (this door is permanently sealed).
E.—Keyhole (hang key on handle).
F. & G.—Wainscoting.
H.—Side of fireplace.
I. & J.—Walls.
K.—Ceilings.
L.—Wireless.
M. & N.—Between floor boards.
Take up carpet or lino.
Fill in, and relay carpet.
O.—Tiles (gas and water pipe entrance and mouseholes).
P.—Ventilator (brown pa[per] and paste).
Outside of house also.
FIREPLACE. Close up chimney with
Q.—Rags or sacks.
R.—Plywood.
S.—Strong brown paper to paste down plywood over fireplace.
T.—Carpet nailed to window, ready to lower for protection against glass splinters, and for use at night, to prevent light showing outside. Battens at side to fasten down if required.
U.—Heavy curtain (will do).
V.—Transparent wrapping or other strong paper to

AIR RAID PRECAUTIONS

ARP

An Album to contain a Series of Cigarette Cards of National Importance

W. D. & H. O. WILLS
BRANCH OF THE IMPERIAL TOBACCO COMPANY (OF GREAT BRITAIN AND IRELAND), LIMITED

PRICE O

How much prote Government's air give? What is b high explosive refuge room b the British pu

During 1937 the Spanish Republicans had been bombed by the German air force; it was evident how much damage could be caused. In November 1937, the Commons voted to build air raid shelters in Britain's towns and cities. By 1938 plans were well advanced for air raid precautions (ARP), and metropolitan boroughs held exhibitions to inform an apprehensive public on what to do and how to cope, and to recruit volunteers as air raid wardens or for first aid posts. Booklets like How To Be Safe from Air Raids could be purchased and Wills issued ARP cigarette cards (above). When the Anderson shelters were issued they cost £7 each to purchase, but were free to families earning less than £250 p.a. Eventually 2¼ million were erected.

4

The ability to identify aircraft as they flew above, and spot the difference between friend and foe, was vital to home defence. For many, enemy aircraft were the closest they came into contact with the enemy, and for children it became something of a game. The modelling of aircraft was encouraged by the patterns included in magazines like Hobbies Weekly and Aero Modeller. Alternatively boxed kits were available. There was a companion volume to the Daily Mirror's 'Spot Them in the Air' which was suited to those who lived by the coast; Spot Them At Sea priced at 6d.

7

"Yes, Dear, we got on all right in the Black-out, but he had to put three layers of tissue-paper over his torch!"

Safety in the Black-out !

? **Why Risk Your Life**

A LITTLE ♥ YOU CAN'T **BLACK-OUT !**

SOMEWHERE IN THE BLACK-OUT !

THEATRE IN BLACK-OUT

THE PLAYHOUSES are emerging from darkness—surely. We wait in our own private darknesses and resurrection. They are indispensable at all times, in p... that ... ury hence, ... re than Ar... histo... guard the... and ... prints, th... Irvi... Siddons... we "made... theat...

"Oh, Girls, I've been kissed in the black-out!"

BLACK-OUT!

"Not A Black-Out-Look!"

A BLACK-OUT'S A BLACK-OUT AND SHE MUST BE TOLD—TO-MORROW.

" PUT THAT BLINKIN' LIGHT OUT !"

OUT NOTICE

I'D LIKE TO BE NEAR YOU IN THE BLACK-OUT.

12 SILHOUETTES

A FRIENDLY ARGUMENT

12 YOUR LIGHT'S SHOWING

11 SILHOUETTES

AIR-RAID WARDEN

The Amusing Topical Card Game

BLACK-OUT!

The Game to cheer you up

EVERYBODY'S PLAYING IT!

YOUR LIGHT'S SHOWING

BLACK-OUT FASHIONS

KATIE'S COSTUME

LOOK OUT IN THE BLACK-OUT

REGULATION WHITE PATCH ON MUDGUARD

GOOD TYRES AND BRAKES

As soon as the black-out began in September 1939, there was a rush to the shops to buy heavy curtain material, blinds, sealing tape and black paint – all of which quickly ran out. Car head lamps were fitted with a slit mask and other lights were dimmed. Even though bumpers were painted white, road deaths increased rapidly; however fewer pedestrians were killed during black-out hours.

8 Romancing in the black-out could be more adventurous.

LEND TO DEFEND HIS RIGHT TO BE FREE

BUY NATIONAL SAVINGS CERTIFICATES

THEY ARE PLANNING THEIR FUTURE. ARE YOU?

SAVE WITH A PLAN

You can	SAVINGS PER DAY	APPROXIMATE SAVINGS AT END OF		
		ONE CALENDAR MONTH	ONE YEAR	TWO YEARS
	4d	£10	£6	£12
	6d	£15	£9	£18
	1:0	£1:10	£18	£36
	2:6	£3:15	£45	£90

NOTE: INTEREST WOULD BE ADDED TO THESE AMOUNTS

THE DAILY POST-WAR CREDIT
INTRODUCED IN JANUARY, 1941
for Men—4d. for Women

POST OFFICE SAVINGS BANK
NATIONAL SAVINGS CERTIFICATES

OF SAVING - ASK THE OFFICER WHO PAYS YOU

BACK THE GREAT ATTACK
with **WAR SAVINGS**

»KEEP ON SAVING«

SALUTE THE SOLDIER

Buy "GANGWAY"
VICTORY BONDS

LEND TO DEFEND THE RIGHT TO BE FREE

BUY NATIONAL SAVINGS CERTIFICATES

THE MOST YOU CAN SAVE IS THE LEAST THEY DESERVE

FORM A

£ SAVINGS GROUP NOW!

CONVOY your COUNTRY to VICTORY
BUY
DEFENCE BONDS
AT BANKS AND POST OFFICES

Posters by eminent artists such as Pat Keely, Tom Purvis, Rowland Hilder, Elgar and John Pimlott helped to encourage the purchase of National Savings Certificates and Victory Bonds.

In the months following the Czechoslovakian crisis of September 1938, 38 million gas masks were issued to adults, children and babies. For small children, look-alike Mickey Mouse masks were deemed to be more friendly, but they were later withdrawn due to the over use of scarce resources. Women found that the obligatory gas mask box doubled up as a handbag in which to carry face powder and other essentials, perhaps the 'see clear' preparation for the gas mask window (see above top). In the event, gas masks were never required, though there was the constant reminder to have them at hand; even in 1943, theatre programmes carried the line 'remember always bring your gas mask' (see page 49). For comic postcards here was something to poke fun at.

don't telephone or telegraph if a letter or postcard will do.

think twice
before making any Trunk-Calls

STOP
WON'T A LETTER OR A POSTCARD DO?

THINK TWICE
BEFORE MAKING A TRUNK CALL

BE BRIEF
BE BRIEF

STOP!
won't a letter or a post-card do?

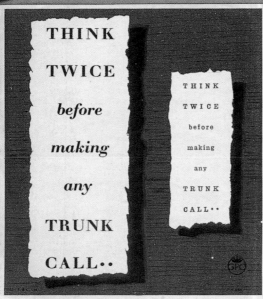

THINK TWICE *before making any* TRUNK CALL··

THINK TWICE before making any TRUNK CALL··

BE BRIEF

STOP
WON'T A LETTER OR POSTCARD DO

Think TWICE
Think TWICE
before making any TRUNK CALL

MAKE THE NATION STRONGER
BANK YOUR SAVINGS
MONEY IN THE SAVINGS BANK IS MONEY LENT TO THE NATION
CAPITAL & INTEREST ARE GUARANTEED
POST OFFICE SAVINGS BANK

DON'T telephone or telegraph if a letter or a post-card will do

'Save, save, save' was the repetitive message on posters, bookmarks and leaflets. Waste paper was constantly needed for the war effort. Don't telephone if a postcard will do – think twice before making a trunk call through the telephone exchange.

12

HOW YOUR SALVAGE HELPS TO MAKE A RESCUE LAUNCH

1 SCRAP METAL
SCRAP IRON NEEDED FOR STEEL HULL. STEEL NEEDED FOR MAKING ENGINE AND MACHINE-GUNS. BRASS MAKES CARTRIDGE CASES. 3-PINT TIN KETTLE MAKES 40 MACHINE-GUN BULLETS. PHOSPHOR BRONZE NEEDED FOR PROPELLOR. COPPER FOR RADIO COMPONENTS

2 ROPE, STRING, TWINE
MAKE NEW SHIP'S ROPE

3 WASTE PAPER
ONE ENVELOPE MAKES 50 WADS FOR MACHINE-GUN CARTRIDGES. TWELVE OLD LETTERS MAKE A CARTRIDGE BOX. WASTE PAPER ALSO MAKES GASKET WASHERS FOR ENGINE AND PROVIDES INSULATION FOR RADIO

4 SCRAP RUBBER
MAKES ELECTRICAL AND RADIO INSULATORS AND COMPONENTS

5 BONES
GIVE GLYCERINE—A COMPONENT IN CORDITE CHARGES FOR MACHINE-GUN CARTRIDGES

6 RAGS
COTTON RAGS MAKE SPECIAL GRADES OF PAPER FOR CHARTS. ALSO ENGINE WIPERS

SAVE IT FOR THE COLLECTOR WHEN HE CALLS

BOROUGH of BRENTFORD and CHISWICK

FIGHT WASTE ALSO!

SCRAP METAL and CLEAN WASTE PAPER

PUT THEM BY YOUR DUSTBIN NOT IN IT

COLLECTED REGULARLY BY THE COUNCIL

SCRAP METAL

LONDON REGION SALVAGE DRIVE — SEPTEMBER 13th to 27th, 1941

Mrs Smith is helping to win the war!

Every London Region housewife can help to win the War by putting out for the Salvage Collector ALL Old Books, Magazines and Paper, ALL Old Metal Ornaments, Tools, Door Knockers, etc., ALL Bones and ALL Rags—they're all needed for vital munitions and supplies. AND, all scraps of Food are wanted, too, to feed the Pigs and Poultry. Bins supplied free to groups of householders.

AND NOW, MAKE EVERY WEEK A SALVAGE WEEK!

BOOKMARK

NOT IN THE DUSTBIN PLEASE!

WASTE PAPER

REFUSE ONLY

YOUR COUNCIL REQUESTS:—

DO NOT PUT CLEAN CARDBOARD & PAPER IN THE DUSTBIN

BOOKMARK

IT'S STILL VITAL!

WASTE PAPER

WAR FACTORIES NEED MORE GAS

How Much Can YOU Save?

---

save fuel
INFORMATION LEAFLET

"LAG" and RELAX!

THE INSULATION OF HOT WATER TANKS AND PIPES

It is ESSENTIAL that we all safeguard our own stocks of coal and coke during the winter, particularly as this is the time of year when a sufficient supply of hot water is a necessity.

You put a tea-cosy over your tea-pot to keep the heat in and the cold out. "Lag" your hot-water tank and pipes and you will be applying the same principle.

BUT there's one great difference : ONCE you have "lagged" your hot water system you don't have to keep on doing it ; you can forget about it.

THREE ADVANTAGES OF "LAGGING"

1 By "lagging" a 25 gallon hot-water tank a TON OR MORE of COAL or COKE will be SAVED in a year.

2 Water in "lagged" tanks and pipes remains hot for a considerable number of hours gone out.

3 Clothes can be aired over danger of their becoming dis

---

save fuel
INFORMATION LEAFLET

HOW TO MAKE BRIQUETTES FROM COAL DUST OR SLACK

is low, there is usually plenty of dust ar r. Good use can be made of this dust an ing" your own briquettes. This leaflet tel

EMENTS FOR MAKING BRIQUETTES

8 to 10 PARTS COAL DUST or SLACK.

1 PART CEMENT.

WATER TO MIX.

1 COAL SHOVEL.

1 FLOWER POT (3 inches across).

at a time, working the mixture from th outside, until the who is quite even and loo like damp earth or like wet clay.

Ram the mixtur tightly into the flow pot, using the sho or a small trowel. Tur out onto the boar With the right amoun of water, the briquet

---

E FOR FUEL

L WASTE ne job leads to EL WANT n another

OKE · GAS · ELECTRICITY · OIL

Keep your clean waste paper (including wrapping paper, pieces of cardboard, large and small cardboard boxes), separate from household refuse and make it into a neat bundle for the Dustman to collect when he calls. You will thus assist your Local Authority to supply raw material to British Industry and so prevent unnecessary imports.

HELP TO REDUCE DISPOSAL COSTS

★ Small pieces of paper and cardboard which will not pack easily can be conveniently put into a large cardboard box or case.

RAW MATERIAL is WAR MATERIAL

if **THEY** starve

THEY CAN LIVE ON WHAT YOU THROW OUT

WE starve

Cattle, pigs, poultry must be fed. Otherwise we shall go even shorter of eggs, milk, bacon, pork and beef.

But - the country is short of feeding stuffs. Imports of feeding products have been drastically cut - because shipping is vitally needed for munitions, aeroplanes, etc.

SAVE YOUR SCRAPS OF FOOD!

SCRAPE THE PLATTER CLEAN— EVERY OUNCE COUNTS

Keep them out of the Keep in a seperate bowl or bu and covered to discourag

It will be collected dai converted into valuable f and cattle.

Remember

Every ounce counts don't throw shipping saved means vital munitions carri

Issued by HEDLEY, BYRNE & Co. Ltd., 11 Wimpole St

Save WASTE PAPER

including wrapping

WASTE PAPER IS URGENTLY NEEDED NOW

WARNING!

Any person **BURNING OR DESTROYING WASTEPAPER**
(WRAPPING PAPER, CARDBOARD BOXES, ENVELOPES, NEWSPAPERS, MAGAZINES, ETC.)

IS GUILTY OF AN OFFENCE AGAINST THE NATIONAL WAR EFFORT

Every scrap is needed for essential national requirements.

Save it for local Council collections.

Week Ending October 24 1942   THREEPENCE

Woman EVERY THURSDAY

SALVAGE

warm woollies for fighting men

To save on imports it was vital for as much food as possible to be grown at home. The Women's Land Army supported the farmers, at their height they numbered some 80,000. Digging for Victory was encouraged in the garden or allotment along with any suitable land, including public parks. By 1943 the number of allotments under cultivation had almost doubled. Much publicity was given to the need for winter growing as well.

8D

Coupon Savers

BLOUSES, SKIRTS
JACKETS, BOLEROS. ETC.

TWO-WAY
BOLERO
& FOUR-WAY
SKIRT
PATTERN

These Blouse Patterns

No. 223
SEPTEMBER 6, 1941
Woman
THREEPENCE

COMPLETE STORY
by Lyn Arnold

NEW EMBROIDERY
in Full Colour

AUTUMN FROCK
in Five Styles

Your Ration Book

WELDON
FASHION SERIES No. 487
Practical Wear
for **WAR WORK**

6D

FREE *inside*
PATTERN of smart
SHIRT and OVERALL

CLOTHING COUPON
QUIZ
2nd Edition Revised

Answers to Questions
on the Rationing of
Clothing, Footwear, Cloth
and Knitting Yarn

Crown Copyright reserved

1942-43 CLOTHING BOOK

This book may not be used until the holder's name, full postal
address and National Registration (Identity Card) Number
have been plainly written below in INK.

NAME
(BLOCK LETTERS) RUTENBERG DANIEL
ADDRESS
(BLOCK LETTERS) 2 GROSVENOR GARDENS
TOWN LONDON SW1 (COUNTY)

NATIONAL REGISTRATION IDENTITY CARD NUMBER

AKBU 192 3 X

Read the instructions within carefully, and take great care not to lose this book

This book is the property of His Majesty's Government.
MOTOR SPIRIT RATION BOOK No.
For the months of AUGUST, SEPTEMBER and OCTOBER, 1940 AF 31839

M/C
NOT EXCEEDING
250 c.c.

Motor Cycle
(including Auto-Cycle)
Registered Number of Vehicle
ECV 889

Date and Office of Issue
LISKEARD 22.40 CORNWALL

The coupons in this book authorise the furnishing
and acquisition of the number of units of motor
spirit specified on the coupons subject to the
conditions appearing thereon.

ANY PERSON FURNISHING OR ACQUIRING
WITH THE CONDITIONS ON WHICH
TO PROSECUTION.

The issue of a Ration Book does not guarantee to
the holder any minimum quantity of motor spirit
and the book may be cancelled at any time with—

MINISTRY OF FOOD
**RATION BOOK
SUPPLEMENT**
This is a Spare Book
**YOU WILL BE TOLD
HOW AND WHEN TO USE IT**

OFFICIAL
PAID

Surname GIBBS
Other Names Mabel
Address Marshfoot
Hailsham

If found, please return to
HAILSHAM, S.E. 33.

FOOD OFFICE.

NATIONAL REGISTRATION NO.
ERNI 91

Food rationing began on
Monday 8 January 1940,
during one of the coldest winters
on record. Petrol rationing was introduced
during September 1940, and by March 1942
petrol was virtually unobtainable for
private use. June 1941 saw clothing rationed.
Some grocers used an ingenious device to
cut out the ration coupons – a pair
of scissors that cut round the
corner of the coupon and 'stabbed' it.
Children could play at rationing with
dolly's ration book and meat ration weigher.

With clothing coupons restricting the number of new purchases to the equivalent of a new outfit every year (the allowance was cut back even further within nine months) hemlines rose as an economy measure and for men double-breasted suits were out and turn-ups removed. 'Make do and mend' was now the order.

Sachets or bottles of liquid silk stockings provided a substitute for the real thing – or gravy browning, with a pencil liner for the seam.

WELDON KNITTING SERIES No. 24

6^d

New WOOLLIES for our SAILORS, SOLDIERS and AIRMEN

Instructions for 20 COMFORT DESIGNS

MEND AND MAKE-DO TO SAVE BUYING NEW

MAKE-DO AND MEND

MAKE DO AND MEND LEAFLET No. 7

PATCHES

Patches are **important**—every one you put on helps you to put off buying something new. And it's just as easy to patch properly as to cobble. Half the battle is knowing how to cut and place your material...

CHART LEAFLET No. 1 ISSUED BY THE BOARD OF TRADE

HOW TO PATCH ELBOWS AND TROUSERS
by Mrs. SEW-and-SEW

CHART LEAFLET No. 4 ISSUED BY THE BOARD OF TRADE

HOW TO PATCH SHEETS AND BLANKETS
by Mrs. Sew-and-Sew

Knitting for the R.A.F.

OFFICIAL BOOK OF INSTRUCTIONS

1/-

ROYAL AIR FORCE Comforts Committee
20 BERKELEY SQ. LONDON. W.I.

HINTS ON WASHING

MAKE DO AND MEND

UNPICK AND KNIT AGAIN

WHERE'S THAT MOTH?

DECORATIVE PATCHES

PREPARED FOR THE BOARD OF TRADE BY THE MINISTRY OF INFORMATION

Price 3^d net

Specially prepared for FINE SILK HOSE 4 PLY 40 Yds.
COL. E65

MAKE DO
COATS CLARK
AND MEND

CHART LEAFLET No. 8 ISSUED BY THE BOARD OF TRADE

HOW TO PATCH A SHIRT
by Mrs. SEW-and-SEW

● Shirts are easy to mend, as the patches can be cut from other parts of the garment. They can be replaced by similar material cut from a discarded shirt, or soft cotton. When the cuffs start to fray, they should be carefully unpicked and reversed. As the are double, the worn edge will then be inside the fold. If you are using new fabric for patching, it should be washed first.

Economy Design SIZE 32. No. 149
9½^d

GREEN VEGETABLES

No country in the world grows vegetables better than we do, and probably no country in the world cooks them worse. For generations we have wasted our root vegetables by excessive peeling and over-cooking, and boiled most of the goodness out of our green vegetables—only to pour it down the sink.

When fresh fruit is short we need green vegetables more than ever because they all contain the important fresh fruit vitamin, Vitamin C. Some have more than others. Brussels Sprouts, parsley and watercress all contain more than orange, cabbage, cauliflower, spinach, swedes, broccoli, turnip tops and kale are all good sources of this vitamin. Not only do green vegetables give us vitamin C, but also vitamins A and B, iron and calcium. Green peas and beans, bread, French and runner, make a welcome change in the menu, but remember they do not take the place of the leafy, green vegetables, as they contain only a little vitamin C. See that you have a salad a day as well as peas and beans when they are in season.

MINISTRY OF FOOD — MF — LEAFLET No. 1

IRENE VEAL suggests some war time CAKES

Some of these recipes were entries in the RADIO TIMES WARTIME CAKE COMPETITION and are re-printed by permission of the Editor of the RADIO TIMES.

'One-pot' meals

Perhaps, like so many people nowadays, you have to cook on one gas-ring, a one-burner stove or an open fire. But there is no reason why you should put up with "scratch" meals. These real two-course meals for four people are planned to be well-balanced, delicious and really practical. Here are seven suggestions.

MEALS without MEAT

Seven appetising meals without using the meat ration

ALL RECIPES FOR 4 PERSONS   ALL SPOONS LEVEL

FOODS TO USE INSTEAD OF MEAT

Meat is a body-building food and can be replaced only by one of the other body-building foods.

1. The best are : Milk (fresh, household or canned), Cheese, Fish (fresh or canned) and Eggs (fresh or dried).

2. Second best are : Soya flour, Dried Peas, Beans and Lentils, Oatmeal and Semolina.

Our bodies use a mixture of the two kinds very well.

MF No. 29

Jam Making and Fruit Bottling

There is still a great shortage of food throughout Europe, and it is vital that everyone should help by growing all they can in gardens and allotments and preserving for winter use.

Home-made jams—"the sort that Mother makes"—and home-grown bottled fruits are the real thing : a source of pride to the housewife and of enjoyment to the family.

Preserve all you can : do not let any fruit be wasted. You will help yourself and help hungry Europe.

Making the most of the meat

Some people like to spread their meat ration over the whole week. Others prefer to use their ration for one good joint on Sunday. In this folder suggestions are made for both plans. For the first week, the meat ration is spread over five days, and off-the-ration dishes are suggested for the other two.

For the second week a roast is served for Sunday, and suggestions are made for off-the-ration dishes for the rest of the week.

D.2.

Defend the Kitchen Front !

A War-time Cookery DEMONSTRATION

will be held at

The C of E School

on

Monday, April 28th 2-30 pm

ADMISSION FREE

In co-operation with the
HERTFORDSHIRE COUNTY COUNCIL

I pass this on to you

SOMETHING FOR TEA

By M J Mathieson

Miss Mathieson is the Secretary of the West Ham Branch of the Women's Gas Council and a Home Service Adviser to the Gas Light & Coke Co. She took her training at the National Training College of Domestic Subjects and holds the Cordon Bleu for cookery.

A spot of Welsh cooking

MADEIRA CAKE WITHOUT SUGAR	CINNAMON BISCUITS
CANADIAN GINGER BREAD	OATMEAL BISCUITS
BAKEWELL TART	CHEESE SCONES
RASPBERRY BUNS	SYRUP SCONES
CHOCOLATE SANDWICH WITH ORANGE CREAM FILLING	DROP SCONES
ORANGE BISCUITS	OATMEAL SCONES

Series B. No. 7   Illustrated by HARRY ROUNTREE

Potato Pete's recipe book

POTATO PETE'S NURSERY RHYMES

Little Jack Horner
Sat in a corner
Eating potato pie.
He took a large bite,
And said with delight
Oh, what a strong boy am I.

Jack Sprat could eat no fat
His wife could eat no lean ;
So they both ate potatoes
And scraped their platters clean.

There was an old woman
She had so many children she didn't know
what to do.
She gave them potatoes instead of some bread,
And the children were happy and very well fed.

HELP TO WIN THE WAR...

IN YOUR KITCHEN

NATURE DOES IT BEST

OFFER OF FREE COOKERY BOOK WITHIN

Try cooking Cabbage this way

LID TIGHTLY ON — COOK FOR 10-15 MINUTES

CABBAGE SHREDDED COARSELY

JUST ENOUGH WATER TO COVER BOTTOM OF PAN

It's twice as delicious

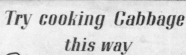

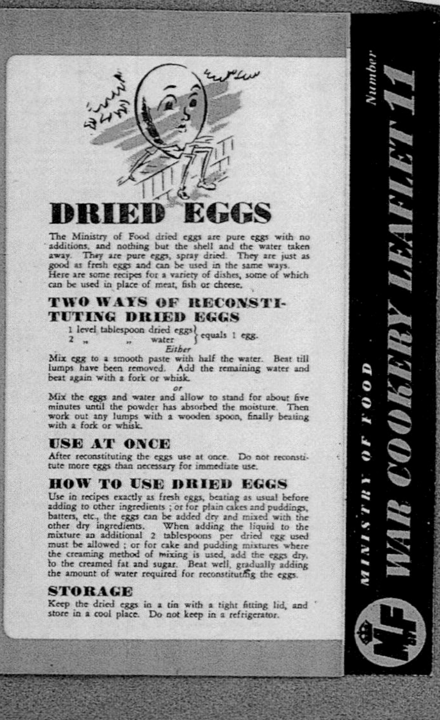

PLEASE SEE OTHER SIDE →

DRIED EGGS

The Ministry of Food dried eggs are pure eggs with no additions and nothing but the shell and the water taken away. They are pure eggs, spray dried. They are just as good as fresh eggs and can be used in the same ways.

TWO WAYS OF RECONSTITUTING DRIED EGGS

1 level, tablespoon dried egg }
2   „   „   water   } equals 1 egg.

Either

Mix egg to a smooth paste with half the water. Beat till lumps have been removed. Add the remaining water and beat again with a fork or whisk.

or

Mix the eggs and water and allow to stand for about five minutes until the powder has absorbed the moisture. Then work out any lumps with a wooden spoon, finally beating with a fork or whisk.

USE AT ONCE

After reconstituting the eggs use at once. Do not reconstitute more eggs than necessary for immediate use.

HOW TO USE DRIED EGGS

Use in recipes exactly as fresh eggs, beating as usual before adding to other ingredients ; or for plain cakes and puddings, batters, etc., the egg can be added dry and mixed with the other dry ingredients. When adding the liquid to the mixture an additional 2 tablespoons per dried egg used must be allowed ; or for cake and pudding mixtures where the creaming method of mixing is used, add the eggs dry, to the creamed fat and sugar. Beat well, gradually adding the amount of water required for reconstituting the eggs.

STORAGE

Keep the dried eggs in a tin with a tight fitting lid, and store in a cool place. Do not keep in a refrigerator.

MF MINISTRY OF FOOD — WAR COOKERY LEAFLET Number 11

Dried Egg RECIPE SLIP D.E.2

HOT BACON AND EGG SALAD (for 4 persons)

2 eggs, reconstituted
1 small cabbage
½ oz. margarine
1 oz. flour
½ pint vegetable liquid
4 teaspoons sugar
1 teaspoon made mustard
Pepper and salt
Vinegar to taste
1 lb. new potatoes, cooked and sliced
2 or 3 carrots, cooked and sliced
1 lb. cooked peas
4 rashers bacon, cooked and chopped
1 onion or clove of garlic, grated

(Please turn over)

Handwritten note:

Much effort was put into schemes for a better-fed nation under conditions of severe rationing. The people's health improved steadily as they ate turnip pie, haricot hotpot and war-and-peace pudding — exotic names covered a multitude of commonplace ingredients. As Gert and Daisy said in their cookery book 'don't forget to make the meal look as nice as you can — there's all the difference between a meal that is nicely dished up and one that is chucked at you, because, as the old song says, "It's not the bit of fish, it's the parsley round the dish that tickles the poor old man!"'

Potatoes were never rationed and Potato Pete was created to promote the extensive variety of potato possibilities. Never before had there been such awareness of nutritional needs.

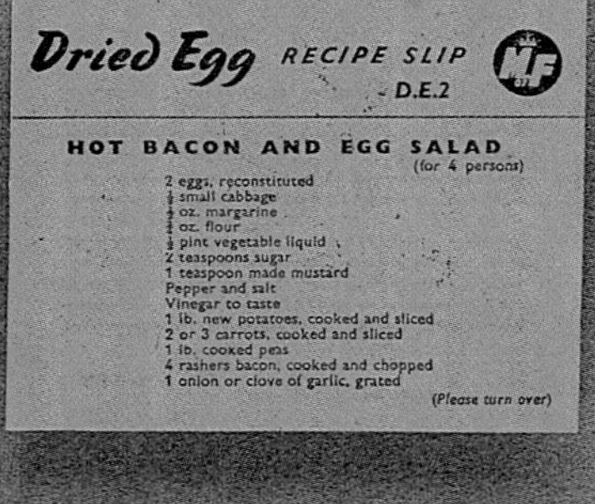

FUEL SAVING IN THE KITCHEN

Hedgerow Harvest

There is a wealth of wild foods in our hedgerows and fields for those who are within reach of the countryside. None of this harvest should be wasted. Here is exceedingly useful here you can gather it in...

MINISTRY OF FOOD — MF — LEAFLET No 5

WHAT TO EAT IN WARTIME

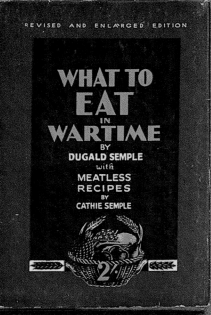

REVISED AND ENLARGED EDITION

WHAT TO EAT IN WARTIME

BY DUGALD SEMPLE

with MEATLESS RECIPES BY CATHIE SEMPLE

2/-

48   WAR TIME COOKERY BOOK

for ½ hour, covering with greaseproof paper when nicely browned.

SHEEP'S HEAD WITH CAPER SAUCE

4 TO 5 PERSONS

1 sheep's head	½ pint milk
2 pints water	1 tablespoonful capers
1 oz. flour	salt and pepper

Method.—Wash the sheep's head thoroughly in salt and water. Place in a pan and add the water. Simmer until tender—about 2 hours. Remove from pan and take out the tongue and the brains and cut the meat from the cheeks. Slice the tongue and the meat and put them with the brains on a dish and keep hot. Take ¼ pint of the stock and ½ pint milk and bring to the boil. Thicken with flour mixed to a paste with milk, and add the capers. Pour this sauce over the meat on the dish and serve.

The remaining stock and the sheep's head bones should be reboiled with the addition of vegetables and barley to make Scotch Broth.

VEGETABLE MARROW WITH LIVER STUFFING

4 TO 5 PERSONS

1 marrow	1 onion
¼ lb. cold cooked liver	1 teaspoonful mixed herbs
¼ lb. breadcrumbs	a little gravy, salt and
2 oz. suet or dripping	pepper

Method.—Peel the marrow, cut in half lengthways, scoop out the seeds. Mince the liver and the onion, add the breadcrumbs, herbs, suet, seasoning, and gravy and mix thoroughly. Stuff the marrow with this mixture and put the halves together. Tie up with tape, wrap in greased paper and bake until the marrow is tender. Serve with brown gravy made from bone stock.

Rations: The answers

Five foods will be rationed

4 oz. IS A WEEK'S RATION FOR ...

DAILY EXPRESS WAR TIME COOKERY BOOK

FIRST FOODS TO BE RATIONED: EXTRA FOR INVALIDS

You MUST follow these rules for your ration book

1/-

F. W. P. CARTER

THE PENGUIN BOOK OF FOOD GROWING STORING and COOKING

Seven suggestions for dinners which need no meat

· 1 ·

Pea vegetable and milk soup. Hard brown bread. Steamed fruit pudding.

· 2 ·

Eggs in savoury white sauce or savoury carrots. Greens. Potatoes. Apple charlotte or baked bread pudding.

· 3 ·

Potato, celery and milk soup. Curried beans and green vegetable.

· 4 ·

Stewed potatoes, oat cakes. Stewed apple pulp, dried or fresh, and cornflour. Glass of milk.

· 5 ·

Fresh or tinned fish, potato, beetroot and cress salad. Milk pudding and jam or sultanas.

· 6 ·

Parsnip, carrot and potato pie, gravy, greens. Bottled plum pulp and custard. Glass of milk.

· 7 ·

Artichoke and potato milk soup. Beetroot, cress, bean and carrot salad with sweetened dressing.

National Wheatmeal bread to be served with each meal.

RATION DINNERS

Homely Savoury Dishes adapted to war conditions for Families & Canteens

2D

Published by THE CENTRAL COUNCIL FOR HEALTH EDUCATION
TAVISTOCK HOUSE, TAVISTOCK SQUARE, LONDON, W.C.1

WARTIME FOOD FOR *Growing* CHILDREN

From the Ministry of Food's KITCHEN FRONT BROADCASTS

FOURPENCE NET.

GERT and DAISY'S WARTIME COOKERY BOOK

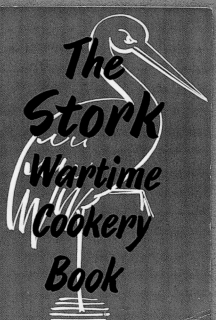

The Stork Wartime Cookery Book

THE KITCHEN FRONT

NATIONAL ROLY-POLY

CRUST	MEAT, ETC.
6 ozs. National flour	6 ozs. cooked mixed vegetables
1 oz. suet	3 ozs. cooked brains
1 oz. grated raw potato	4 ozs. minced beef
1 teaspoonful baking powder	
Pinch of salt	
Water to mix	

FOR CRUST : Rub the fat into the flour, add the baking powder, salt and grated raw potato. Mix to a stiff dough with cold water (it might take a little more water than usual). Roll out and your dough is ready.

FOR FILLING : Cream all filling ingredients together, spread on your rolled-out dough, roll up as usual and either steam it for an hour and a half, or bake it in a moderate oven for 40 minutes to 1 hour. If you are steaming, wrap the pudding in a floured cloth. If you are baking, roll it in oatmeal. You will find the oatmeal will toast a most succulent brown.

RABBIT STEW WITH PRUNE DUMPLINGS

1 rabbit	1 tablespoonful dripping
1 bay leaf	2 tablespoonsful flour
2—3 large carrots	Salt and pepper. Water.

FOR THE DUMPLINGS :

8 cooked prunes (they should not be too soft)	
6 ozs. flour	1 oz. lard or cooking fat
½ teaspoonful salt	

Put the jointed rabbit and the carrots, sliced, into a saucepan with the bay leaf and a seasoning of salt and pepper. Cover with water and bring to the boil. Remove all scum, then simmer gently for 1 hour. Strain off ½ of a pint of the liquor. Melt the dripping, add the flour and blend thoroughly. Stir in the boiling hot liquor to make a smooth thickened sauce. Put back the rabbit and the carrots.

To make the dumplings, rub the fat into the flour and salt, moisten with enough cold water to make a soft dough. Roll out and divide into 8 pieces. Wrap a stoned prune in each piece. Mould into little dumplings, drop into fast boiling salted water and cook quickly for 8—10 minutes. Skim them up and put them in with the rabbit and carrot. Serve at once.

22

The KITCHEN FRONT

122 WARTIME RECIPES

broadcast by Frederick Grisewood, Mabel Constanduros and others, specially selected by the Ministry of Food.

6D. NET

FOOD FACTS FOR THE KITCHEN FRONT

A Book of Wartime Recipes and Hints

WITH A FOREWORD BY LORD WOOLTON

Price Sixpence

A KITCHEN GOES TO WAR

FAMOUS PEOPLE Contribute 150 Recipes to A RATION-TIME COOKERY BOOK

Meat and Poultry

MOSTLY UNRATIONED

M. GABRIEL VALLET, Maître Chef de Cuisine, Grosvenor House.

BRAINS FRITTO

2 sets calves' brains.

METHOD : Cook the brains in salted water, adding a drop of vinegar. Allow to cool, then cut in pieces and dip in batter.¹ Fry in smoking hot fat or oil, drain well and serve with tomato sauce.

HELEN SIMPSON says her dish requires a good heart.

CABBAGE STUFFED WITH SAUSAGE MEAT

METHOD : Take a fresh cabbage with, as far as you can feel, a good heart. Cut away the outer leaves. With a pointed knife with a serrated blade and cut ...

... fish-well ... any ... stock, ...

... Arthur Webb, on page 108, tells how to make ... ed batter.

35

GOOD HOUSEKEEPING BOOK OF **Thrifty War-Time Recipes**

Economical Vegetable, Fish, Meat & Game Dishes
Soups and Salads

Approved by the MINISTRY OF FOOD

6D

A 100 WARTIME CHEESE RECIPES

A HUNDRED CHEESE RECIPES

By Ivan Baker

The Housewife's help in the use of her cheese ration

Ninepence

A 100 WARTIME CHEESE RECIPES

A well stocked larder! Most brands survived, some were replaced like Stork margarine with National margarine. Breakfast cereals were 'zoned' so that only one brand was obtainable in an allocated part of the country. Packaging was modified to save on raw materials, putting on their 'wartime jackets' (see Orlox suet top shelf centre) which meant using poorer quality card, reducing the width of the label, replacing metal stoppers with glass

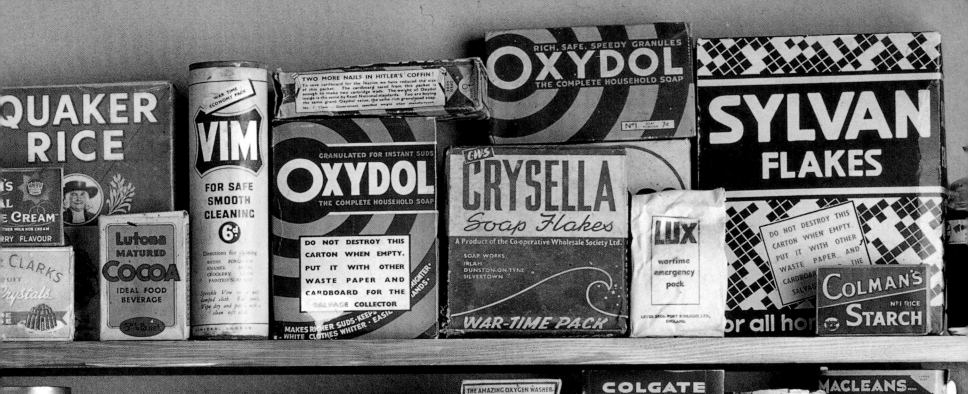

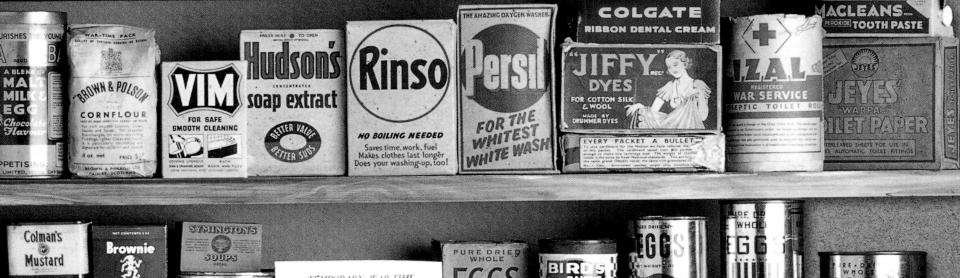

or cork, using glass bottles instead of tin (as with Brasso) or card boxes instead of tin (as with ¼ lb cocoa packs) and using less printing ink. Consumers were urged "not to destroy this carton when empty. Put it out with other waste paper and cardboard for the salvage collector". Oxydol "put two more nails in Hitler's coffin" each time a pack was salvaged as two cartridge wads could be made. Tea canisters became 'gas proof' and Teafusa claimed to extend the ration.

IT'S CHOCOLATE IT'S **FOOD**

IT'S **CADBURY'S**

The nation's sweet tooth had to contend with the rationing of confectionery from July 1942. An allocation of points to everyone restricted sweet consumption to 3oz per head per week. Wrappers and price cards indicated the controlled price and category into which a product fell. The lack of full-cream milk meant that separated milk was used, and the result was termed 'blended chocolate'. The familiar red wrapper of the Kit Kat bar turned to blue, indicating that it was now plain chocolate.

Many wrappers were eventually made from grease-proof paper, such as Oliver Twist and Cadbury's Ration. Advertising display cards were in short supply and shopkeepers hung on to pre-war examples to fill their emptying shop windows. Adverts became topical; 'Got your gas mask? Got your Bassetts?' was the question inside an air raid shelter.

"Tell that Spy it's no good tapping the wire for 15 minutes — explain I'm just enjoying a CHURCHMAN'S Nº1"

Send him his favourite Brand

DUTY FREE
CIGARETTES AND TOBACCOS
FOR THE TROOPS IN FRANCE

| PLAYERS GOLD FLAKE CRAVEN "A" | 120 for 3/9 |
| WOODBINES STAR WEIGHTS TENNERS | 150 for 3/4 |

FREDK WRIGHT
LTD. TOBACCONISTS SINCE 19

WICH & NORW

DUTY FREE CIGARETTES FOR **H.M. FORCES SERVING IN FRANCE**

OR NAVAL PERSONNEL SERVING IN SEA GOING SHIPS IN COMMISSION

USE THE ORDER FORM OVERLEAF

28th SEPTEMBER 1939.

19, RED LION STREET. HOLBORN. W.C.1.

NOTICE.

Shopkeepers who have increased prices of Tobacco etc are gross and flagrant PROFITEERS. They are charging extra on OLD stocks at OLD prices. Therefore ROBBING the public who are already heavily burdened

BUY BRITISH FROM BRITISH AND BE BRITISH.

G WELLESLEY SHAW

CHURCHMAN'S Nº1 Special VIRGINIA CIGARETTES

Rothmans **Pall Mall**
By Special Appointment
WAR EMERGENCY
Blended with a small percentage of Oriental Tobaccos. ROTHMANS LTD.
ROTHMANS. L.D. 5 & 5ª.Pall Mall. LONDON. S.W.

Cigarettes and tobacco were considered to be morale-boosters during the war, and although restricted, continued to be available — queues formed quickly when a shop delivery had been made. Cigarette cards stopped being issued with the outbreak of war and advertising showcards all but ceased in order to save on cardboard. As the war progressed, cigarette packs began to be made from flimsy paper wrappers and using less ink. The familiar designs were replaced by a continuous repetitive strip of the brand name. As Virginia tobacco began to run low, the supply was supplemented by blending in about 2% of Oriental tobacco (usually Turkish). The Pall Mall tin above has a 'war emergency' label that notifies the customer of this change. Labels around the tobacco tins were reduced in width and some tins carried a request for their return to the tobacconist. Match boxes urged smokers to 'use matches sparingly'. As in the Great War, sending tobacco or cigarettes to troops serving overseas was seen as a patriotic gesture, and gratefully received by those at the other end.

SCOTTIS BELL MATCHES — USE MATCHES SPARINGLY
CAPT. WEBB — BRYANT & MAY LTD — USE MATCHES SPARINGLY
STARLIGHT — WASTE NOT WANT NOT — BRITISH MATCHES
BE LIKE DAD KEEP MUM
EN GLO — S.J.MORELAN GLO — FIVE WORDS TO... BER WHEN DOING... JOB OF WORK... THIS WAR... "IT ALL DEPE... ON ME!"
THE SMOKER'S MATCH — SWAN VESTAS — USE MATCHES SPARINGLY — BRITISH MADE
PILOT MATCH — USE MATCHES SPARINGLY — SUPPORT HOME INDUSTRIES
USE MATCHES SPARINGLY — BRYANT & MAY'S BRYMAY SPECIAL SAFETY MATCH — 27 PRIZE MEDALS
BOOK MATCHES Best Quality
SPITFIRE MATCHES

PLAYER'S NAVY CUT
"THREE NUNS" TOBACCO "NONE NICER"
PLAYERS
R.E.G DARK EMPIRE SHAG
C.W.S LINDEN HONEY DEW TOBACCO
MEDIUM STRENGTH "CAPSTAN" Navy Cut
PLAYER'S "MEDIUM" NAVY CUT

THE TEST OF A SOLDIER —

is to keep his mouth shut when he would look big if he told what he knew

PRINTED FOR H.M. STATIONERY OFFICE BY 57™ M...

Keep mum
she's not so dumb!

CARELESS TALK COSTS LIVES

Printed for H.M. Stationery Office by Greycaine Ltd., Watford and London. 51-101

TELLING a friend may

mean telling **THE ENEMY**

PRINTED FOR H.M. STATIONERY OFFICE BY J. WEINER LTD., LONDON, W.C.1 51-9265

" .... but for Heaven's sake don't say *I* told you!"

CARELESS TALK
COSTS LIVES

'Careless talk costs lives' was a slogan in constant use during the campaign to make people aware that 'walls had ears', and so it seems did everyone else. fougasse (C.K. Bird) illustrated the posters (right and above) where Hitler & Co appear to listen in.

"Of course there's no ... in your knowing ...

You never k... who's listening

CARE... COST...

Propaganda messages were mostly evident on posters, in the high street, the town hall, libraries and at railway stations, but they could also be found on milk bottle tops and bus tickets, match boxes and stickers attached to postal envelopes. Many cartons had their own hidden exhortations to save the packaging for the salvage collector.

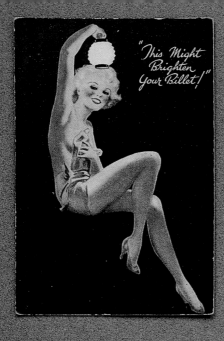

"This Might Brighten Your Billet!"

"'ERE, CAN'T YOU READ?"

GENTLEMEN GENTLEMEN

Though they ration petrol, tea or meat
I swear by Heaven above,

They never will or can control
That sloppy thing called 'Love'!

WHEN CAN WE "MEAT" AGAIN?

"He grabbed my ration-book, Officer, and tried to pinch my Personal Points!"

WHO WANTS BLINKING SEARCHLIGHTS TO-NIGHT?

A "BAMFORTH" COMIC

"A blow on the Siegfried line!"

"You an' your go to bed early to save coal an' light!!"

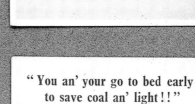

"WE HAD AN ESCAPED GERMAN PRISONER HIDING IN OUR HOUSE LAST NIGHT!"
"HOW DID YOU KNOW?"
"I HEARD MUM TELL DAD THERE WAS A JERRY UNDER THE BED!"

I GOT HER WITH A PARCEL OF SOLDIERS' COMFORTS, SIR!

A "BAMFORTH" COMIC

"HAVE THESE CHILDREN BEEN EVACUATED?"
"NOT YET SIR—I'M JUST MIXING THEM UP A DOSE!"

CHILDRENS WELFARE

IT'S ALL BECAUSE OF HITLER
YOUR SUGAR RATION'S LITTLER!
IT'S ALL BECAUSE OF HITLER
THE COST OF MILD AND BITTER!
IT'S ALL BECAUSE OF HITLER
THE PETROL RATION'S HIT YER!

BUT REMEMBER THIS, MY FRIEND,
WHEN AT NIGHT YOU GROPE ABOUT,
ADOLF'S GOING TO PAY FOR THIS---
HIS LIGHT WILL BE PUT OUT!

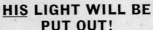

NOW—CAN I COVER MY TOES—OR BLOW MY NOSE?

This man of froth
once wrote a book
And called the tripe,
"Mein Kampf,"
But now we know,
he named it wrong,
It should have been
"Mein Ramp."

To see the doom
of this Nazi spark
Hold this card to
the light and look
in the dark.

"This Front is quite Active!"

GLORIOUS STALINGRAD.

PULL

The comic postcard provided a good laugh as well as a convenient form of communication. All the pre-war artists, especially Donald McGill and Mabel Lucie Attwell, were on hand to create their miniature masterpieces.

The postcard on the right was luminous and in the dark showed Hitlers skeleton. On the left, in the mechanical postcard, a Russian soldier punches Hitler whose hands go up in surrender. Hitler was the butt of many jokes, but so were the black-out, rationing, gas masks, shortages and the jerry under the bed.

"Are we good? I ask you, how the blazes could we be otherwise in all this clobber?"

LOOK AT THAT, YOU FOOL---AND **YOU** MADE AN **AIR RAID WARDEN** THIS MORNING!

Maid: "The siren's gone. Missus says you've to go in the dug-out!"
Lodger: "I won't, the cistern's not working!"

YOUR UNITS MUST NOT BE DISCLOSED!

JOLLY UNSPORTSMANLIKE I CALL IT!

"I wish to offer you my apologies, Gentlemen,--- I have sometimes referred to the Nazis as Swine!"

"I WISH I'D COME HERE BEFORE THE WAR!"
"NICE OF YOU TO SAY THAT, SIR!"
"NICE MI EYE! THIS BLUE PENCIL EGG MIGHT HAVE BEEN FRESH THEN!"

"WAS THAT A BOMB?"
"NO,—IT WAS ONLY ME."

"WOOL WITHOUT COUPONS!"

KEEP IT DARK—
I'LL BE SEEING YOU SOON!

DON'T LET SUCH THINGS WORRY YOU---

THINGS ARE NEVER AS BAD AS THEY SEEM!
WHY THE "DEUCE" NEED WE WORRY IF WE PLAY THE GAME, OLD BEAN!

I'M TELLING YOU!

IF HITLER WANTS ANY MORE TERRITORY

HE CAN HAVE **MINE!**

N.B.G. COMMERCIAL TRAVELLER

GOSH! I WISH I'D ONE O' THEM DICTATORS HERE---
JUST FOR TWO MINUTES!

IT WON'T BE ALL SMOOTH GOING—WE'LL JUST HAVE TO GO CAUTIOUSLY FOR A TIME!

"Lummy, if I got 'old of him, I'd tear 'is Swastika off!"
"My! Ain't you bloodthirsty!"

"There's two chaps I'd like to give a kick in the pants. Hitler an' that ruddy Quarter bloke!"
"Why, what's Hitler done?"

WITH THE HOME GUARD

" ADVANCE FRIEND AND BE RECOGNISED"

PHOTOCHROM COPYRIGHT.   HOME GUARD SILHOUETTES. No. 2

The morale of the fighting forces suffered if they did not receive regular mail from home, and those on the home front were encouraged to "do your duty" especially at Christmas time. Greetings cards were readily adapted to the mood of the moment, and Valentines had service men and women in mind, "for Valentine and Victory".

For B.F.s

DOUGLAS.

HOME FRONT LINES

DAVID LANGDON

GRABBERWOCKY
and Other Fights of Fancy

BASS PALE ALE

By MICHAEL BARSLEY

ILLUSTRATED BY OSBERT LANCASTER

SECOND PRINTING

ALICE IN WUNDERGROUND
and Other Blits and Pi...

WUNDERGROUND

Written and Illustrated
By MICHAEL BARSLEY

Author of
...berwocky and Other Fights of Fanc...

R·A·F'ing it

by
"L.A.C. ERRANT"
SKETCHES BY EDGAR NORFIELD

FREDERICK MULLER LTD
LONDON

BEHI... SPIT...

by
RAFF

Who's the boy-friend in khaki, who is he
Whom girls to-day would like for company?
Not always the brass-hat,
The R. S. M., or some big shot like that;
You'll find that they are mostly well content
With what the gods have sent—
Just Tommy in his battle-dress and cap,
A splendid sort of chap,
Care-free and gay, not over-flushed with pay,
But generous with his bob or two a day;
No high-brow stuff,
But, when the need is, tough;
Fit as a fiddle, loyal to his pals,
And golly! what a gallant with the gals!
Here's the boy-friend in khaki, here is he
Whom girls to-day find such good company.

GREEN LINE

Laurie Taylor

When Jack comes home from chasing
The swift Italian fleet,
He'll once again be pacing
High road or busy street
(He seems to find it bracing)
With something rather sweet!
Perhaps her hair is WAVY,
She's trim and ship-shape too,
And that attracts the Navy,
Those jolly lads in blue,
Who are such handy-men, we know,
At winning hearts where'er they go!

THIS ENGLAND
1940
ILLUSTRATED BY LOW

Watching and waiting the long hours through,
Watching and waiting, Fritz, for you!
Called in the night to leave my bed
[Those sirens are fit to wake the dead],
Called in the day-time from work and play—
Off to the roof-top, up and away!
Watching in sunshine, in rain, or in fog
[What couldn't I do to a stiff glass of grog?]
Braving the dangers that lurk in the sky
[Whether from bombers or birds as they fly],
Soaking or freezing or scorching like hell—
I find myself wishing that Hitler as well
Could taste the delights of a fire-watching spell!

Look out!

Laugh It Off

TUCK BOOK

EUROPE SINCE VERSAILLES
by
LOW

PUNCH on the HOME FRONT

"INVERNESS NEXT STOP, LADY"
ACANTHUS

Stories and 150 Drawings from "Punch"
2/- NET

Humour was an essential part of
survival on the home front.
Newspapers and magazines carried
regular cartoons, and there were
many special booklets full of
cartoons that took the lid off
life in the forces, the Home Guard,
or war-stressed civilian life.

ARPIES AND SIRENS

SP

R

D

SP

W

CD

THE A B C OF CIVIL DEFENCE

A is the Ambulance picking up bits,
B is for Black-out, for Bomb and for Blitz,
C is Control that copes with the trouble,
D, Demolition that digs in the rubble,
E is Equipment (mask and tin hat),
F for Fire Service, First-aid-and-all-that,
G, poison Gases that worry our noses,
H for fire Hatchets, for Hydrants and Hoses,
I's for Incendiaries (all mess and fuss),
J is for Jerry who drops them on us,
K is our Knitting, patient row upon row,
L is for London and Lights we mayn't show,
M, Mobile Units that dash in and out,
N for the Nurses they carry about,
O is for Ominous Overhead humming,
P, Purple Warnings that tell us they're coming,
Q for the Questions on Gas and First-aid,
R, Rescue Party, Respirator and Raid,
S is for Searchlights, raking the Stars,
T for the Telephone, calling all cars,
U is the Uniform screening our charms,
V is our Version of last night's alarms,
W for Warning, for Warden and War,
X for explosives that are more than a bore,
Y is the Civil Defence Youth-and-beauty,
Z is the Zeal which they spend on their duty.

ACCORDING TO PLA...
Armengol's war cartoons

SECON... SPOTLI...

BEING THE SECOND BOOK OF "SPOT...
WAR CARTOONS REPRINTED FROM "T...
BRISTOL "EVENING WORLD" IN AID OF...
★ BRISTOL'S OWN FUND ★
WITH A SUMMARY OF FOUR MO...

34

The young pilots of the RAF, flying their Spitfires and Hurricanes in the skies over Britain were perhaps the most highly-visible heroes of all. With their Brylcreemed hair and good looks, it was little wonder that they were used to promote such diverse products as toothpaste and cocoa. During the Battle of Britain in August 1940, Churchill paid tribute to the RAF fighter pilots "Never in the field of human conflict was so much owed by so many to so few."

BOMBER COMMAND

BOMBER COMMAND CONTINUES

COASTAL COMMAND

THE ADMIRALTY ACCOUNT OF NAVAL OPER

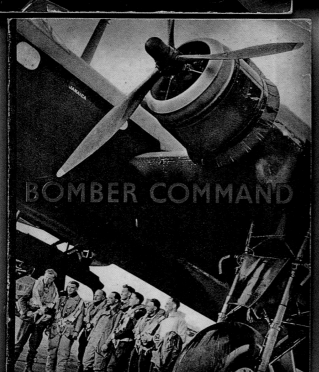

BOMBER COMMAND

FRONT LINE
1940-1941

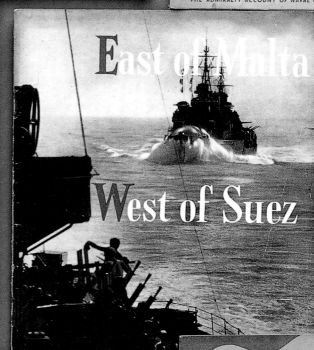

East of Malta

West of Suez

"WINGS OF EMPIRE"

INDIA AND BURMA SQUADRONS OF THE R.A.F.

A WORKER'S DAY
UNDER GERMAN OCCUPATION

WITH A FOREWORD BY JIM

Transport goes to War

THE School

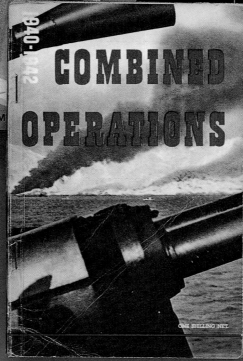

940-1942

COMBINED OPERATIONS

ONE SHILLING NET

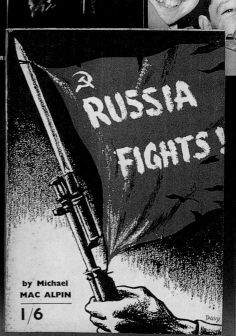

RUSSIA FIGHTS!

by Michael MAC ALPIN

1/6

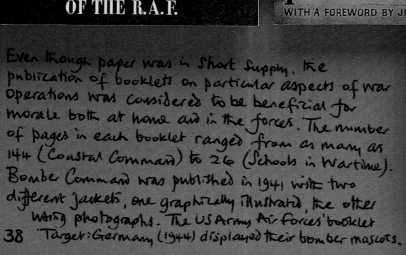

Even though paper was in short supply, the
publication of booklets on particular aspects of war
operations was considered to be beneficial for
morale both at home and in the forces. The number
of pages in each booklet ranged from as many as
144 (Coastal Command) to 26 (Schools in Wartime).
Bomber Command was published in 1941 with two
different jackets, one graphically illustrated, the other
using photographs. The US Army Air Forces' booklet
38   Target: Germany (1944) displayed their bomber mascots.

THE EIGHTH ARMY

1/6 Net

JANUARY 1943

FLEET AIR ARM

THE ROYAL ARMOURED CORPS

THROUGH MUD & BLOOD TO THE GREEN FIELDS BEYOND

ROOF OVER BRITAIN

THE OFFICIAL STORY OF THE A.A DEFENCES, 1939–1942

A. GAMES

NINEPENCE NET

HIS MAJESTY'S MINESWEEPERS

NINEPENCE

THE POST OFFICE

EUROPE

MIDDLE EAST

FAR EAST

1/3 NET

WENT TO WAR

EPIC WAR

WARTIME

FIGHTING PAPPY

ROYAL FLUSH

"Impatient Virgin"

HOLY MACKEREL

"TIN HUSSY"

Sleepytime Girl

SHOOT LUKE

Piccadilly

WHAM BAM

54 BAT OUTA HELL

Sloppy

The Eagles Wrath

OLE SWAY

MAN POWER

THE STORY OF BRITAIN'S MOBILISATION FOR WAR

EPIC OF NGRAD

BY STREET CORNER

BBONS
R CORRESPONDENT
S.S.R.

6D

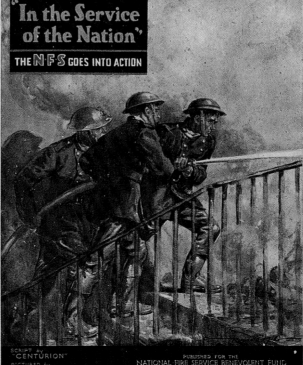
TARGET: GERMANY

The U.S. Army Air Forces' official story of the
VIII Bomber Command's first year over Europe

ONE SHILLING AND SIXPENCE NET

"In the Service
of the Nation"

THE N·F·S GOES INTO ACTION

SCRIPT BY
"CENTURION"
PICTURED BY
FIREMAN REGINALD MILLS

PUBLISHED FOR THE
NATIONAL FIRE SERVICE BENEVOLENT FUND
By RAPHAEL TUCK & SONS LTD

HIS MAJESTY'S

SUBMARINES

NINEPENCE NET

LITTLE HOME-MADE GIFTS for XMAS See Inside

MY HOME
9.d
XMAS 1941

The W.A.A.F.

for NEEDLEWORK, KNITTING & CROCHET inside

MAN and HOME
& GOOD NEEDLEWORK Magazine

WOMAN'S OWN

3.d
ON SALE FRIDAY
JUNE 25th 1943

H.M.S.

GIRL'S OWN

FEBRUARY 1943
9.d
IN CANADA 20 Cents

Spotlight on Service

A.T.S.

W.A.A.F.

I'M A FIREGIRL

ITER RIGHTER TEETH

KOLYNOS
DENTAL CREAM

KOLYNOS

GIRL'S OWN

2/2 1/3 & 7½
INCLUDING

THE ECONO

LIFE IN THE A.T.S.

NOVEMBER

Everywoman
AND WOMAN'S FAIR

The MORRIS OWNER

A.R.P. POST

ARP

MO 1939

1943
9.d

Women's magazine
covers promoted the
glamorous life of women
in uniform, the three
main services being the
ATS, WAAF and WRNS.
Books like We Serve (1941)
helped back up these ideals;
the film The Gentle Sex
(1943) followed the lives of
seven women who joined
the Auxiliary Territorial
Service. In every facet of
service life, women played
key roles, whether driving
cars or lorries, ferrying
aircraft from factory to
RAF base, ciphering messages,
being mechanics or
meteorologists.

41

WOMEN OF BRITAIN
COME INTO THE FACTORIES

ASK AT ANY EMPLOYMENT EXCHANGE FOR ADVICE AND FULL DETAILS

PRINTED FOR H.M. STATIONERY OFFICE BY LOWE & BRYDONE PRINTERS LTD. LONDON. N.W.10. 51-2171

Wartime work for many was gruelling and some of the hardest was in the factories. Women had to shorten their hair to avoid it becoming entangled in the machinery. Radio programmes like Music While You Work and Workers Playtime (begun in May 1941 and broadcast three times a week from a different canteen each time) kept up the community spirit. The booklet Our Wonderful Women commented, "A new and precious unity has arisen which the far-sighted hail as infinite progress and none has contributed more to this transfiguration than the women of Britain. This is total war and every man, woman and child is potentially in the front line."

ER GARDENS
MALVERN
★
MAMMOTH
WHIST
DRIVE
Organised by the Streets Savings Groups

**MALVERN
ELCOME HOME
FUND**

d by the Chairman of the Malvern Urban District
ouncil (Major W. J. C. Kendall, M.C., J.P.)
+
Subscription will be gratefully
received

MALVERN U.D.C.

BOOKS
PERIODICALS
MAGAZINES

0,000 ARE WANTED
FOR
E SERVICES (R.N., ARMY, R.A.F., M.N)
General Montgomery has said of the 8th Army :
Tell everyone to send them something to read.
That's what they want something to read."

NITIONS
he Mosquito Aircraft has a large proportion
of paper in its construction.

TZED LIBRARIES
50,000 Volumes were destroyed in the raids
on Coventry alone.

The PLAN
road to
BERLIN

MAY
8-15
1943

MALVERN
Wings
for Victory
WEEK

WINGS FOR VICTORY

OFFICIAL PROGRAMME 3d.

'A BIT OF HOME'

SPITFIRE FUND
& EMPIRE PROPAGANDA STAMPS
THE
BRITISH EMPIRE
STANDS FOR
WORLD PEACE
AND
SECURITY
DEFEND IT
TELL
THE
WORLD
OUR
AIMS
MORE
& MORE
PLANES
ESSENTIAL
ALL ASKED TO HELP
24 STAMPS 1/-
HALF SPITFIRES
HALF PROPAGANDA
Constitutional Publishing Co. 42. Maiden Lane-Strand. w.c.2.

SPITFIRE
FUND
7.86

Help the Spitfire-Fund

The manufacturers and
distributors of this brooch...
BROOCH
1/6
MADE IN
ENGLAND

FINEST GILT

BRITISH MADE

RED CROSS & St JOHN
needs your help for
Prisoners of War

CARLTON and DISTRICT
WAR WEAPONS' WEEK
July 19th — 26th
1941

OUR
£100,000
Twenty Spitfires
CARLTON CALLS TO ITS CITIZENS
LEND TO THE LIMIT

Official Souvenir Pro...

POST CARD
ON ACTIVE
SERVICE
This parcel of Cigarettes
has been presented by

HELP
HINA

AR

please help-

PLEASE HELP CHINA

BUY WAR BONDS

YOUR CITY'S
BOMBER FUND

You can help in this War
By giving to the
DAILY
SKETCH
WAR RELIEF FUND
to provide the Forces with
CIGARETTES, GAMES AND COMFORTS
The Fund is under the distinguished patronage of the leaders of
our Fighting Services

The Rt. Hon.
LORD CHATFIELD
Minister of Defence

The Rt. Hon.
WINSTON CHURCHILL
First Lord of the
Admiralty

The Rt. Hon.
L. HORE-BELISHA
Secretary of State
for War

The Rt. Hon.
SIR KINGSLEY WOOD
Secretary of State
for Air

ORLEYWOOD URBAN DISTRICT
S FOR VICTORY WEEK

ednesday, May 12th
HILDREN'S
cy Dress Parade
(Open to all)
SLE LOWER ROAD, C— W— 5.15 p.m.
(THE GARAGE)
S—1. Decorated Bicycles.
2. "Wings for Victory."
    Ages—(1) under 7 years.
          (2) 7 to 11 years.
          (3) 11 to 14 years and over.
3. Group—e.g., Britannia and
    her Attendants, etc.

ORLEYWOOD BOOK APPEAL!
JULY 24th to AUGUST 7th, 1943

Chorleywood Residents are asked to find
10,000
BOOKS AND PERIODICALS
DURING THE FORTNIGHT OF THIS APPEAL
The purpose being :
o provide reading matter for our Armed Forces
in England and abroad (including our boys who
are Prisoners of War, and our Merchant Navy).
o re-stock blitzed Libraries.
o ensure preservation of valuable books for
posterity by careful scrutiny of every volume.
o provide material for munitions of war.
is one of the most earnest appeals yet directed
horleywood - the books will be a direct gift from
our war effort.
through your bookshelves and cupboards and

SHIP HALFPENNIES
Royal Naval War Libraries
(REGISTERED UNDER THE WAR CHARITIES ACT 1940.)

HALF
PENNY
1940

PLEASE
COLLECT YOURS
for US
and communicate with :
ROYAL NAVAL WAR LIBRARIES
40, WILLIAM IV. STREET,
LONDON, W.C.2.
TELEPHONE : TEMPLE BAR 2011.
Every Halfpenny helps to buy
BOOKS FOR SAILORS

Birmingham
Strikes Back !

Contented—thanks to
THE RED CROSS LIBRARY
EVERY week the Red Cross and St. John
War Organisation Headquarters Library
distributes more than 5,000 books and
magazines to naval establishments, military hospitals, civil
hospitals, and hospital ships at home and
abroad. Since the outbreak of war over 2,000
libraries have been established by the Red
Cross, and over 900,000 books and magazines
have been distributed by the Headquarters
Library and its County Depots. Books are

EIGHT MILLION POUNDS
wanted extra savings from
Birmingham and Solihull

atriotic Picture Postcards
IN AID OF
The Daily Sketch
WAR RELIEF FUND
THE RIGHT HON
NEVILLE CHAMBERLAIN
THE RIGHT HON.
WINSTON CHURCHILL
THE RIGHT HON.
L. HORE BELISHA
6
Postcards
1/-
GENERAL LORD GORT
GENERAL GAMELIN
SIR CYRIL NEWALL
COMFORTS FOR THE FIGHTING FORCES

ONE PENNY
GOES TO THE FUND
THE RIGHT HON.
WINSTON CHURCHILL
PATRIOTIC POSTCARD
IN AID OF
The Daily Sketch
WAR RELIEF FUND

ONE PENNY
GOES TO THE FUND
"PEACE WITH HONOUR"
THE RIGHT HON.
NEVILLE CHAMBERLAIN
PATRIOTIC POSTCARD
IN AID OF
The Daily Sketch
WAR RELIEF FUND

Flag-days, concerts and whist drives all
raised funds. Appeals were launched to help Russia, China and
France. Books were wanted for those in the services and for
blitzed libraries. The Spitfire fund was particularly successful—
by spring of 1941 £13m had been raised (a Spitfire "cost £5,000").

(We're Gonna Hang Out) THE WASHING ON THE SIEGFRIED LINE
BY JIMMY KENNEDY & MICHAEL CARR

FEATURED WITH ENORMOUS SUCCESS BY FLORRIE FORDE

IN THE MOOD
THE "JITTERBUG" CRAZE.
Words by ANDY RAZAF
Music by JOE GARLAND

FULL INSTRUCTIONS AND ILLUSTRATIONS
THE "JITTERBUG" DANCE ON BACK
(BALLROOM ROUTINE DEVISED BY MISS A.)

Featured by
GLENN MILLER
AND HIS ORCHESTRA.
(Recorded on H.M.V. B.D. 5565).

THE WHITE CLIFFS OF

UKULELE, GUITAR AND ACCORDION ACC.

FEATURED AND BROADCAST BY Bebe

LONDON - ENGLAND
B. FELDMAN
125-9 SHAFTESBURY
NEW YORK: SHAPIRO BERNS

RUN, RABBIT - RUN!
Words by NOEL GAY & RALPH BUTLER
Music by NOEL GAY
From
The Little Dog laughed

Berlin or Bust
(THE SLOGAN OF THE B.E.F.)
Words & Music by
ROSS PARKER and HUGHIE CHARLES

HITLER'S MEIN KAMPF

CREATED BY JACK PAYNE AND HIS BAND

Irwin Dash Music Co Ltd
17, BERNERS ST, LONDON, W.1.
Put DASH in your Programmes

THE A.R.P.
SONG

WE'LL MEET AGAIN
Words & Music by
ROSS PARKER and HUGHIE CHARLES

FEATURED & BROADCAST BY
JOE LOSS
AND HIS BAND

Irwin Dash Music Co Ltd
17, BERNERS ST, LONDON, W.1
Put DASH in your Programmes

6D

I shall be waiting
Words & Music by
ROSS PARKER
HUGHIE CHARLES
and JOE IRWIN

FEATURED & BROADCAST BY
SYD LIPTON
AND HIS GROSVENOR HOUSE DANCE BAND

Irwin Dash Music Co Ltd
17, BERNERS ST, LONDON, W.1.
Put DASH in your Programmes

6D NET

THEY CAN'T RATION

SUNG WITH ENORMOUS SUCCESS BY
BETTY DRIVER

MUSIC
23 DENMARK

LORDS of the AIR

WORDS & MUSIC

GOODMORNING SERGEANT MAJOR

WORDS
ART I

PRAISE THE LORD and PASS THE AMMUNITION

The phrase "Praise the Lord and pass the ammunition" was used by Chaplain Howell Forgy to encourage men passing ammunition during the Japanese air attack on Pearl Harbour

THE MAN WITH THE BIG CIGAR

CHORUS
Oh, the man with the big cigar,
He's our empire's lucky star
Like Wellington and Nelson
He'll show 'em who we are.
His name is Winston Churchill
One of the best is he,
Soldier, Sailor, Statesman,
He'll lead to Victory.
Oh, the man with the big cigar,
He will guide this country far,
For he's a jolly good fellow,
The man with the big cigar.

by
JACK GODARD
NAT TRAVERS &
WILL HAMMER

ROLAND'S PIANOFORTE TUTOR · THE BEST IN THE WORLD
ENGLISH FINGERING   CONTINENTAL FINGERING

THANKS, MISTER ROOSEVELT

MUSIC CO · LTD · 2·3 & 4

UKULELE
PIANO-A

When they sound the last 'ALL CLEAR'

BY HUGH CHARLES   &   LOUIS ELTON

ENTIRE PROCEEDS WILL BE DEVOTED TO ACK-ACK WELFARE THROUGH "THE DAILY SKETCH" WAR RELIEF FUND

THE "ACK-ACK" SONG
VOCAL MARCH

M OF BRITAIN'S ANTI-AIRCRAFT DEFENDERS — FEATURED
E B·B·C· FAMOUS "ACK-ACK"-BEER-BEER PROGRAMME

WHEN THE LIGHTS GO ON AGAIN
(ALL OVER THE WORLD)
BY
EDDIE SEILER
SOL MARCUS
BENNIE BENJEMEN

BY
MY KENNEDY

Composed
NG

LONDON
B. FELD
135-9 SHAFT
AUSTRALASIAN AGE
SYDNEY, MELBOUR

RECORDED & BROADCAST BY
VERA LYNN

The Royalties from the sale of this Song will be paid to the A.T.S. Welfare.

MARCH of the A.T.S

OVE

JIMMY
WILL
FRE

1/-

"ETCH" WAR RELIEF FUND BY   Kennedy Music Co., Ltd.,
36, SOHO SQUARE, LONDON, W.1.
Selling Agents
Campbell, Connelly & Co., Ltd.,
10, DENMARK STREET, LONDON, W.C.2.

Come and have a Drink
AT THE VICTORY ARMS'

Song
WRITTEN & C
JIMMY

A good sing-song in the pub or the air raid shelter kept up morale — and the tradition of community singing. At the outset of war Run, Rabbit, Run! happened to be a popular song by Bud Flanagan — Hitler soon took the place of the rabbit. The ARP Song (above middle) was written and composed (but not illustrated) by King George VI.

47

RADIO TIMES SUPPLEMENTARY ISSUE, September 4, 1939, Vol. 64, No. 831A

Price Twopence

RADIO TIMES
JOURNAL OF THE BRITISH BROADCASTING CORPORATION
(INCORPORATING WORLD-RADIO)

REVISED PROGRAMMES for Sept. 4-10

BROADCASTING CARRIES ON

Radio Times, June 5, 1942. Vol. 75. No. 975. Registered at the G.P.O. as a Newspaper

PRICE TWOPENCE

RADIO TIMES
...ISH BROADCASTING CORPORATION
...ORATING WORLD-RADIO)

PROGRAMMES FOR
June 7—13

PRICE SIXPENCE

KEEP IT GOING!

THE RADIO ALLOTMENT

In this London garden twenty-three different types of vegetables are being grown, as well as a large variety of herbs. Once a week its progress is broadcast to gardeners all over the country.

SIX months ago, in a certain London square, there was little to be heard but the wind blowing, little to be seen but the green grass growing...

PICTURE
and Film Pictorial

Radio Times, May 28, 1943. Vol. 79. No. 1026. Registered at the G.P.O. as a Newspaper

PRICE TWOPENCE

PROGRAMMES FOR
May 30—June 5

RADIO TIMES
JOURNAL OF THE BRITISH BROADCASTING CORPORATION
(INCORPORATING WORLD-RADIO)

This Week

Poison Party
Leon M. Lion plays the lead in *Hemlock for Eight*, the radio play by Clifford Bax on Sunday afternoon, in which...

Elgar and Beethoven
On Wednesday night Sir Adrian Boult will...

WORKERS' PLAYTIME

On Tuesday the second anniversary of this popular show is celebrated with a bumper broadcast affair lasting a whole hour and is also featured in the special 'Workers' Gala Night' programme the same evening. Above are Bill Gates, genial Master of Ceremonies, and the pianists Bruce Merryl (left) and George Myddleton.

ON May 31, 1941, George Myddleton and Jack Clarke sat down at two pianos in a factory canteen and first played the signature tune of 'Workers' Playtime.'...

ELIZABETH FORSTER

Pictur...
Incorporating
Film W...

Radio Times, October 20, 1939. Vol. 65. No. 838. Registered at the G.P.O. as a Newspaper

PRICE TWOPENCE

PROGRAMMES FOR
October 22—28

RADIO TIMES
JOURNAL OF THE BRITISH BROADCASTING CORPORAT...
(INCORPORATING WORLD-RADIO)

A new 'Radio Times' picture of 'Big-Hearted' Arthur Askey and 'Stinker' Richard Murdoch

'Band Waggon, perhaps the most popular
programme of all...' Sir Samuel Hoare in the House of Commons, October 11, 1939

Ministry of Information

(MoI) **FILM Shows**

Programmes of sound films produced for and acquired by the Ministry of Information can be shown anywhere in the country by 16mm. mobile film units. An operator is in charge of the unit, which consists of a screen, sound projector and a car. This tells you...

WHAT TO ... WANT A SHOW →

THEATRE IN BLACK-OUT

THE PLAYHOUSES are emerging from darkness—emerging slowly but surely. We wait in our own private darknesses and wish them a speedy resurrection. They are indispensable at all times, in peace and war. It is unthinkable that anyone, a quarter of a century hence, will be able to write that in his childhood there were no theatres, opening "more than Arabian paradises." At such a time there will be many who will wish to guard the treasures of theatrical history, deriving more than common pleasure from the prints, the books, the playbills and the relics which store memories of Garrick, Mrs. Siddons, Mrs. Jordan, Kean, Irving, Ellen Terry and all the other great actors who have "made the pulse of a crowded theatre beat like that of one man."

WE'RE CO...
THERE'S NOTHIN...

SUNG BY PET...

FROM THE PARA...
"ARF A M..."
PRODUCED BY...

...RDS BY
...R BERNARD

PETER...

Olivia de HAVILLAND

Radio Times, May 17, 1940. Vol 67. No. 868. Registered at the G.P.O. as a Newspaper

PRICE TWOPENCE

PROGRAMMES FOR
May 19—25

RADIO TIMES
JOURNAL OF THE BRITISH BROADCASTING CORPORATION
(INCORPORATING WORLD-RADIO)

On the Air
This Week!

During the coming week your radio will bring you another dazzling array of favourite stars. Here are a few of them.

Flanagan and Allen will be heard on Sunday (Forces programme) in a charity Variety show from Worthing. They will also broadcast again on Saturday in a Star Variety show from...

Leslie Henson, Binnie Hale, Sydney Howard, and Phyllis Robins are four of the artists from the two Firth Shephard shows now running in the West End, *Shephard's Pie* and *Up and Doing*, who will take part in another Sunday broadcast in the Forces programme, called 'Shephard's Flock'.

Robert Montgomery and Jessie Matthews will broadcast on Monday in a special ENSA Half-Hour.

Jimmy O'Dea, the popular Irish comedian, is to be chief fun-maker in a new weekly Variety serial feature, 'Melody and Co.', which will start on Thursday.

Full details of all these broadcasts will be found in the programme pages.

ROBERT MONTGOMERY

JESSIE MATTHEWS

BINNIE HALE

FLANAGAN and ALLEN

LESLIE HENSON

PHYLLIS ROBINS

JIMMY O'DEA

SYDNEY HOWARD

CINEGRAM No. 78

One Penny

Q PLANES

TATLER THEATRE
CHARING CROSS ROAD   GERrard 4815

SECOND PROGRAMME
Friday, November 21st, 1941.

THE

**Gaumont British
Picture Corporation**
LIMITED

in association with the

**SOVIET WAR NEWS
FILM AGENCY**
FILM SECTION OF THE PRESS DEPT.
OF THE SOVIET EMBASSY

Prices: 1|10 : 2|6 : 4|6

**ANGLO-SOVIET
FILM SEASON**

Programme   -   Twopence

The BBC broadcasts were an essential part of the home front day. They became the focal point for much of family life, a source of information. Light music and entertainment, with comedy shows like ITMA (It's That Man Again) featuring Tommy Handley, Band Wagon (a pre-war revival) with Arthur Askey, and Hi, Gang! with Bebe Daniels, Vic Oliver and Ben Lyon. A surprising hit was The Brains Trust that had a regular audience of 11 million. But it was the news that everyone waited for. Maintenance of your radio set was essential; even so by the middle of 1942 about one in every ten sets had broken down.

The cinema was one place to escape from the war. The US film industry was still releasing its usual stream of movies: Gone With the Wind (1939), Pinocchio (1940), The Great Dictator (1940), Citizen Kane (1941), The Road to Zanzibar (1941), Dumbo (1941), Bambi (1942). During 1942 two British films were released: the forces sweetheart, Vera Lynn, made We'll Meet Again and Flanagan & Allen appeared in We'll Smile Again.

Lampooned by cartoonists, Hitler and his cronies were made fun of at every opportunity. Jokes were often lavatorial, and well-known books were parodied, becoming popular sellers (Adolf in Blunderland had reached its fourth edition three months after publication in December 1939). Funds from the sales of Struwwelhitler, a parody on the popular Struwwelpeter, went to the Daily Sketch War Relief Fund which supplied woollen comforts to the Services and food to the victims of air raids. Miniature chamber pots, or 'jerries', were a novelty.

THE BEANO Comic

THE RAINBOW 2²
Tiger Tim's Weekly

SUN

TRIUMPH 2d Every Tuesday
ALL TOGETHER BOYS! WE WANT THE TRIUMPH! CAN YOU HEAR US, NEWSAGENTS?

THE TRIUMPH AND GEM
2d

VOL. XXVIII. No 9 SEPTEMBER 1943

MECCANO MAGAZINE

DON'T WASTE PAPER — COLLECT

THE HOTSPUR
No 484 · FEBRUARY 26th · 1944 PRICE

BOY'S OWN

TINY TOTS (Once a Fortnight) 2d
"Tiny Tots is a Lovely Paper!"

Tiny Tots AND THE SUNBEAM 2d
No. 688. Tuesday. (Once a Fortnight)
WEEK ENDING JULY 19th, 1941.
AND TOT PLAY IN THE PARK.

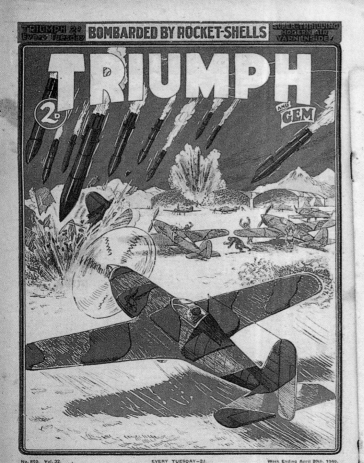

TRIUMPH 2d Every Tuesday BOMBARDED BY ROCKET-SHELLS SUPER-THRILLING MODERN AIR YARN INSIDE

TRIUMPH AND GEM
2d

No. 800. Vol. 32. EVERY TUESDAY—2d. Week Ending April 20th, 1940.

ROCKFIST ROGAN. R.A.F.
No. 1,185. Vol. 4th. Every Friday. Week Ending October 14, 1944.

THE CHAMPION
AND TRIUMPH
3d

LEADER OF THE LOST COMMANDOS.

BOY'S OWN

BLOOD MONEY: By Wilfrid Tremelle
AIR STORIES 9d

Comics for younger children did not dwell
on the realities of war, but for older
children the glamorous side of battle was there in all its glory. By the end of 1942
the size of Meccano Magazine and Boys Own Paper had been halved in size to save
on paper. Doubtless the stories of heroes and articles like 'Are you fit for
flying?' made youngsters look forward to active service. The Wizard contained
the war exploits of Iceberg Bill and The Champion the exploits of Rockfist Rogan of
52 the RAF. Readers of Girls Crystal were treated to 'Alone against the Invader'.

BOY'S OWN PAPER

JANUARY, 1942

No. 472
Vol. 19
EVERY
FRIDAY

GIRLS' CRYSTAL

3ᴰ

AND THE SCHOOLGIRL

Week
Ending
Nov. 4th,
1944.

ALONE AGAINST THE INVADERS

A Girl's War-time Adventures On A Lonely Pacific Island Are Featured In This Thrilling Complete Story—By AUDREY NICHOLLS

WHEN DANGER THREATENED

STORIES OF POWER—AND PEP—AND PUNCH!
A BUNCH OF THE BEST IN THE BEST OF THE BUNCH!

NO. 996
NOV. 30TH
1940

EVERY
MONDAY
2ᴰ

ADVENTURE

FOLKS WITH FADS!

THE MAGNET — THRILLING DETECTIVE-ADVENTURE YARN OF GREYFRIAR

The Magnet

2ᴰ

Week Ending July 15, 1944.
No. 1,172. Vol. 46. Every Friday.

MEET COLWYN DANE, DETECTIVE, INSIDE

THE CHAMPION

3ᴰ

AND TRIUMPH

LEADER OF THE LOST COMMANDOS

WAR-FLYING FICTION OF TO-DAY

AIR STORIES

7ᴰ

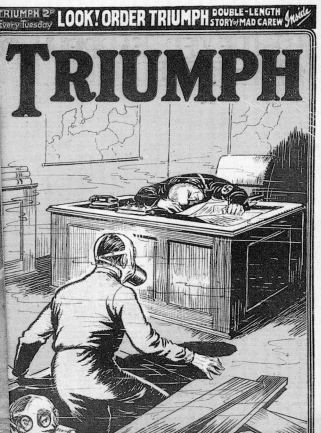

TRIUMPH 2ᴰ
Every Tuesday

LOOK! ORDER TRIUMPH DOUBLE-LENGTH
STORY OF MAD CAREW Inside

TRIUMPH

MEET YOUR
RADIO STARS

FLANAGAN & ALLEN — WILL FYFFE — SANDY POWELL — ARTHUR ASKEY — REVNELL & WEST and 5 OTHERS INSIDE!

RADIO FUN

2ᴰ

BIG-HEARTED

No. 34. June 3rd.

VOL. XXIX. No. 9
SEPTEMBER 1944

MECCANO MAGAZINE

AFTER THE TEST FLIGHT

6ᴰ

BOY'S OWN PAPER

A scene from
"THE SECRET OF ROSMERSTRAND"
(beginning inside)

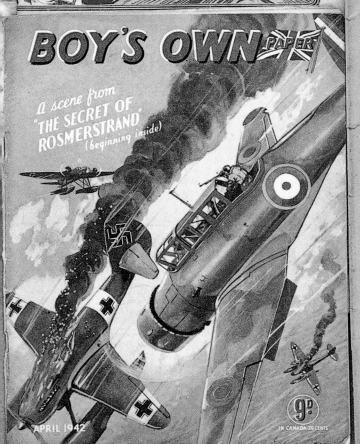

APRIL 1942

9ᴰ

IN CANADA 20 CENTS

"BRITAIN'S SECRET WEAPON" ATTACKED FROM THE AIR!

THE ROVER

No. 935—MAR. 16th, 1940. EVERY THURSDAY 2ᴰ

LOOK OUT FOR NEWS OF MORE

THE WIZARD

No. 1042
JAN. 22ⁿᵈ 1944
PRICE 2ᴰ

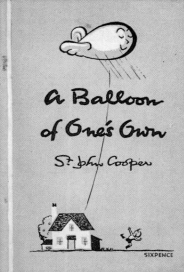

A vast array of child-friendly publications covered many topics of the war. Railways in Wartime showed the Underground being used as an air raid shelter (where over 170,000 people regularly sought refuge), Richmal Crompton's William created his ARP junior branch and Horace visited the BBC (during the war newsreaders gave their name before reading the news in case of impersonation. Barrage balloons were made into friendly anthropomorphic creatures that had their own adventures, such as Bulgy, who had a crew of ten men to look after him as he guarded a brand new factory. "The workmen say that they are doing 'Hush-Hush' work. It is of course very important, and when I find out what it is I shall not be able to tell anyone."

Toy manufacturers devised war-related games to while away the long black-out evenings; jigsaws depicted the latest military skirmish or one of the war leaders. If throwing darts at Hitler's face became boring, you could 'Decorate Goering' by closing your eyes and pinning medals on his chest (in the same way as Pinning the tail on the donkey).

The Battle of the River Plate in December 1939 created an early opportunity for one enterprising firm to devise 'the greatest naval game ever known'; a wooden ship was fired at with a torpedo, scoring points according to the hit – a central hit released the turret. Monopoly's metal counters were replaced by card & wood substitutes, the dice by a complex card spinner.

GERMANS PUT OUT THE NEWS EVERYONE HOPES IS TRUE
Drum-roll heroics—then the build-up of hero-leader fighting to his last breath

'HITLER IS DEAD'

Doenitz goes on radio: I am your new Fuhrer

OBITUARY

THE Daily Express rejoices to announce the report of Adolf Hitler's death. It prints today every line of information

It gives no picture of the world's most hated face.

It records that Hitler was

Victory night—

Daily Mail

NO. 15,290   ONE PENNY ★★★ FOR KING AND EMPIRE   **VICTORY EDITION**   **TUESday FIELD-DAY**   TUESDAY, MAY 8, 1945

3 POWERS WILL ANNOUNCE GREAT SURRENDER SIMULTANEOUSLY

VE-DAY—IT'S ALL OVER

The King to speak to Empire: Victorious generals will follow Premier on radio

Joy-day throngs stop traffic

IN NEW YORK

From Daily Mail Correspondent
New York, Monday.

NEW YORK went wild with excitement when the first unofficial victory report was released. Within a few minutes more than a million people were out in the streets celebrating.

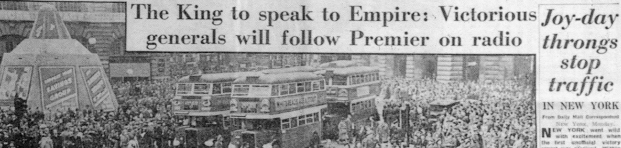

NEWS CHRONICLE, Tuesday, May 7, 1945

VICTORY ISSUE
May 8, 1945

News Chronicle

No. 30,881   TUESDAY, MAY 8, 1945 • ONE PENNY

TODAY IS V DAY

Churchill speaks at 3 p.m., the King at 9; Today and tomorrow are national holidays

TODAY IS V DAY
MORROW IS
PUBLIC HOLIDA
THIS WAS
FOLLOWING OF

"It is understo
accordance with arra
tween the three Grea
official announcemen
broadcast by the Prim
three o'clock tomorro
May 8.

"In view of this fa
Tuesday, will be treat
in Europe Day and
garded as a holida
following, May 9, w
holiday.

"His Majesty th
broadcast to the pe
British Empire and Co
tomorrow at 9 p.m.

"Parliament will
usual time tomorrow.

THANKSGIV

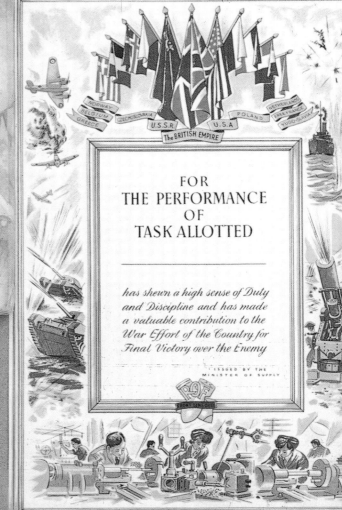

VICTORY CUT-OUT BOOK

DEAN

FOR THE PERFORMANCE OF TASK ALLOTTED

has shewn a high sense of Duty and Discipline and has made a valuable contribution to the War Effort of the Country for Final Victory over the Enemy

ISSUED BY THE
MINISTER OF SUPPLY

Peace was declared on 8 May 1945 (VE Day) - it was all over and spontaneous celebrations ensued; thousands of bonfires were lit, many burning effigies of Hitler. There were street parties, singing, dancing and fancy dress parades. Churchill spoke from Downing Street to the nation, ending "The German war is therefore at an end". Every available mug was quickly pressed into service as a victory souvenir. Victory in Japan followed on 16 August '45 (VJ day) By the time of the official celebrations on 8 June 1946, a few more souvenirs had been produced like silk scarves and a cut-out book.